Lovers, Liars, Conjurers and Thieves

Lovers, Liars, Conjurers and Thieves

Raman Mundair

PEEPAL TREE

First published in Great Britain in 2003
Peepal Tree Press Ltd
17 King's Avenue
Leeds LS6 1QS

ISBN 1-900715-80-5

Cover photograph by Parminder Sekhon

for
S, B and m

Acknowledgements

Acknowledgements are due to the editors of the following publications in which earlier drafts of several poems from this collection have appeared: *The Fire People* (Payback Press, 1998), *Bittersweet* (The Women's Press, 1998), *The Redbeck Anthology of British South Asian Poetry* (Redbeck Press, 1999) and *The New Shetlander.*

I would like to thank the following: Jeremy Poynting for his discerning, precise, editorial eye and his commitment to publishing new poets. Parminder Sekhon for the kind use of her photograph. Hannah Bannister for her design skills. The British Council Literature Dept., the British Council Sweden, and the Dept. of English, Stockholm University, for the writing residency that offered me the invaluable time I needed to complete this collection. The Dept. of English and Drama, Loughborough University and Shetland Arts Trust for their support of my work. Kwame Dawes and Jacob Ross for their invaluable feedback at the early stages of this collection.

Special thanks to my family and friends for their belief in me, and their abundant gifts of love, support, and encouragement: Dodger, Syreeta, Patience, Dorothy, Vaishali, Qing Ling, Max, Sunny, Jess, Yasmin, and the Lindblads.

Contents

Lovers

Liars

Conjurers

Thieves

Lovers

The Folds of my Mother's Sari

Seeded in desperation
I blossomed secreted
in the folds
of my mother's trousseau sari,
gifted from Simla Auntie
who later brought *ghur*
to sweeten my mouth.
My father's crow-like sisters,
diminished by years of strict
fraternal rule, rise and decree
that my mother continuously
drudge to cleanse their ancestral home –
the increase in my mother's belly
put down to an inbred sloth
-fulness, an overindulgence
of their family's rations.
As the sisters,
harped incessantly to
hungry kith and kin
about the insufferable burden
of acquiring a meagre sister-
in-law, who was afflicted
with both lack of grace and dowry,
my mother, silently blissful
in containing the one thing
they could not yet touch,
the one thing she claimed as her own,
bound me closer into her skin.

II

Suckled by an unknown breast
I awoke.
As is custom
the first *dudh* to pass my lips
was not my mother's own.
A neighbour took
my sultana body
and coaxed my lips
to clamp aroused
around my first
object of desire.

III

My father's village:
Khotaran, a mile or so
down from the disused textile
track that ferried fabric
from the mills at Phagwara
to the metropole of Delhi.
My father's ancestry:
a stretch of fertile land
intoxicated with *bhang*.
Remnants of my childhood self:
trunked into a musty, shuttered
room on the roof of a modest
court-yarded house.
The trunk has been prised
many times in my absence
and no one knows for sure
where my silver baby's goblet,
wrapped in my mother's old sari,
has gone, nor the delicate

silver filigree frock, hand stitched
for my first birthday.
Centuries of communal
living have wiped away
all individual claims for self
and Khotaran Aunty says
all the ones with any sense
have long left and only
the fools now remain.
I linger, imprinting in the
footsteps I once made.

Osmosis

My mother
cross-legged on the floor,
a *paraat* of fresh *methay*
in front of her.

Me
small and slithery enough
to squeeze through
the hook of her
working arms
and fingers plucking
succulent leaves
from the stem.

My head
resting on her
shalwared thighs
feeling warmth
oozing through her
skin to skin.

Watching sweet, fragrant
methay fall like angels
into the *paraat*,
knowing that soon there will be
fresh *parathay* with *methay* inside
and *ghee* melting
into its crevices,
and *dhai,* served in small metal bowls
with indentations that sing
like steel musical drums.

Stirrings, nestlings,
I turn my face
towards her special place,
the one where the greatest warmth
glows, where scent roots me
and leaves me with desires
of burying myself deep inside.

Awakening,
my hands
coyly identifying my own special place
'What are you doing?'
My mother's hands stop,
her eyes fix on mine.
'*Ki kar di hai?*'
My hand wavers and works
its way back up.
I say, calmly, clearly,
'It feels good, mummy,
it feels real nice,
when I touch myself
here.'

I watch her face.
She does not falter.
Her face fills with warm colour,
her mouth widens.
She eases me off her *godi*
and, smiling, says
'You naughty girl.
Go and play.'

Name Journeys

Like Rama I have felt the wilderness
but I have not been blessed

with a companion as sweet as she,
Sita; loyal, pure and true of heart.

Like her I have been chastened
through trial by fire. Sita and I,

spiritual sari-sisters entwined
in an infinite silk that would swathe

Draupadi's blush. My name
a journey between rough and smooth,

an interlacing of banyan leaves with sugar
cane. Woven tapestries of journeys;

travelling from South
to North, where the Punjabi in my mouth

became dislodged as milk teeth fell
and hit infertile English soil.

My mouth toiled to accommodate
the rough musicality of Mancunian vowels

and my name became a stumble
that filled English mouths

with a discordant rhyme, an exotic
rhythm dulled, my voice a mystery

in the Anglo echo chamber –
void of history and memory.

Refractions

Minotaur hot in pursuit, I crawl
lost in catacombs, no
silk thread or bread
crumbs to guide me,
no beam of light
to signal a safe home
-coming, in every mirror
cruel reflections.
I am on a bad trip
dissolving; I shrink
and obscure my size
in a way that would make Alice proud.
But no Wonderland here,
only a Snow White vision. I try
to assimilate, skipping
the *Little House on the Prairie* walk,
trying not to stand on the lines
and touching wood.
I lend myself bleached,
willing to the bone-raw,
blistered voice
unused to dialogue, broken
Punjabi jammed Bollywood Hindi
fused into a calcified
internal loop-de-loop
'*Meray jhutay hai Japani,*
Pantaloon hai Englishstani,
Sir pai lal topi Russi
Phir bhi dhil hai Hindustani…'
Through *Janet and John*
and *Wide Range Readers*,
I glean survival essentials
Thank you Thank you
Very much Very much

Please   Please
Sorry, so sorry…
Is this the queue?
But now tell me, how
do you say that which can not be spoken
in any language? How do you say
I think I do not exist?
How do you speak,
where there are no images
of self to claim?

Excuses for a Father

Did you hate yourself in an abrasive country,
with elastic-band open arms, which snapped your back double?
Is that why you tried so hard to erase me
child of your flesh in union with my mother? We two women
scripted into an inevitable, circular dialogue, void of words.
Lights
Camera
Action!
Brass ashtrays fresh from your fingertips gravitate towards my
          magnetic teeth.
Plate glass tables with sharp fake mahogany edges razor off layers
          of my skin.
Your hands, flailing like an acid-crazed Ravana.

Papa, in a world that made you feel like nothing,
how far did you have to go so that you could feel something,
feel something, something, anything?
Papa? How far did you have to go to make those head voices
sing in syncopated harmony?

Papa, I hear that you have a wild dance
which begins with all sorts of unclarities falling
from your mouth like remnants of rubbish thrown in an over-full city bin.
Like semen born from porn you go shooting off
to places no-one else has time for
you and your obscenities.
I hear, daddy, you dance a strange dance now
spiralling into hardwood doors, collapsing onto floors
melting into a 90% proof stupour
vapour from your mouth rising like steam from fresh crapped faeces
while you force your hands to fuse with your head over and over
knocking them in harder, harder,   harder
Is there anyone in?
Papa?   Daddy?   Father?

Do you feel unloved? Un-cared for? Unsafe?
But there are no other hands but yours that torment
your body as it batters chaos into the terror-cemented walls,
of your semi-detached, suburban home.
And Papa, Daddy, Father,
as your golden boy returns to the house of his birth
and speaks his un-cultural truths with his six foot four inch body
against your (in my freeze-framed memory) built like shit-house
        five foot eight,
and as your heir, the carrier of your name in a brood 'unluckily' peppered
        with girl children
that you tried so hard to abort
slams his 6 pack torso un-giving,
against your unrelenting stockpile of wasting flesh,
do you feel something?
Feel something, something, anything?
Who touched you last, Papa? When did you last get held?
Hugged? Stroked?
When did your flesh ever give pleasure, not pain?
And as you feel your 17 year old son's power rising and his
        uncompassionate slam-dunk
passionate defence of his long-flown beloved sister, mother
Do you feel?
Do you feel?
Do you feel?
Do you feel?
Shame.

Body Memories

I do not feel
the sun, but I see it, I cannot hear
the rain, but it covers me.
Sun and rain fill my pores
I could drown
e
  a
    s
      i
        l
          y.
            Smells.
     Sounds.
          Scenes.
Dé
   jà
        vu
I can smell his
fist tearing through
the air
homing its way
into my skin.
I hear my hair
being tugged at the root,
pulled and stretched
across the floor
the weight of my body
following behind it.
I see my consciousness
fade in and out
then flicker
hi tech
     audio visual
         shutdown.

I flirt with
near death experiences,
watch in slow motion
the movement of his mass
on her body.
I absorb the texture of her life
as abrasive grey carpet fibres
work their way into her mouth.
My transcendental fingertips
acknowledge the grooves
imprinted on her cheek
where his thick metal
watchstrap has been indented
proof of forced contact
against her skin
against her will.
I know that she can
almost see the sun
when she twists her neck
towards the window,
narrowing her eyes,
staring at its glaring
yellow light
so that she can create
rainbows that fill her
head with a riot-
ous kaleidoscope.

The Red Chamber

London   winter
ice   freezing
over   cracks
pour   boiling
water   snap
my heart in   pieces
blood   chambers red
clavicle   blood red
vain   journey
I am a maid   in waiting
forever   anticipation
I crave for concrete to make contact
with my skin at 120mph
so that I can feel the relief
like letting the piss-shit go.
It's over
the pain has officially left the building.
Ladies and gentlemen,
experience the high of surviving over and over and over
and over again.
Let me introduce myself,
I am your plastic, fantastic lover,
I can take anything you give me and, baby,
I never die
I am a cat with 90 lives
living   forever
feelings long forgotten,
hidden in the biology
of my body   I am
imaging veins, arteries, heart
pumping, flushing through H^2O
diluting blood weak red,

body 95% liquid, other materials
negligible.
Cry me a river
better still, puncture this weak flesh
let me over-spill, leak, leave
wet patches
that I can lie about (in) later
whilst I tell myself that joy
may split me wide open.
The fear of being undone
on earth as it is in heaven,
I am disbelief in creation.
Reminding myself that we need
to
      fall
            apart
                  to see how strong
                            we are.

Is it like dis-
secting?
Cut-
ting   open
            flesh
to see how it works
so we can learn
to save other
human beings only
it's too late for this
poor,   ripped up
piece of flesh.

A beat resounds
through this blood
red chamber.
Heart beat
rhythm keeps time

echo deafening killing space thick
like phosphorous a mess   I am
covered in blood sticky
redness menstruating
from every orifice leaking
colour into the magnetic
tidal dance cycles
turn,
spin   pirouette
stamp!
Catch the essence
of my breath in the arch
of my back, in the movement
of my hands, extend outwards – give
retract inwards – pull the needle
dart poison straight
through my heart   red blood
red
I am your angelmartyrwitchwhore – too magical
for words project onto me your everything. Memories
are sharp knives inside me, I hide
them under designer clothes.
They rip me up,
shred me, cut through the expense
of living   hiding
a bloody memory
masking emotion
I am sitting on an overfull suitcase
compress
suppress
repress
depress
oppress

Walking Wounded

Inside my body there's a war going on
Seemingly invisible to your eyes
Slashed, knifed in the back, cuts weeping raw
Trailing bloody footprints across your floor
I am the walking wounded

You step neatly out of my way
Safe in knowing what's 'your shit and what's mine'
Seemingly invisible to your eyes
Inside my body there is a war going on
And the bodycount rises

My deaths have been silent and unmemoried
Little girls with their tongues cut out plague my dreams
You step neatly out of my way
Trailing bloody footprints across your floor
You are the walking wounded

Inside my body there's a war going on
Seemingly invisible to your eyes
Confronting you with your blood on my face again
You step neatly out of my way
Safe in knowing what's 'your shit and what's mine'.

Inside my body there's a war going on
Seemingly invisible to your eyes
Slashed, knifed in the back, cuts weeping raw
Trailing bloody footprints across your floor
We are the walking wounded

The Red Chamber Revisited

The dry purple redness fascinates
me, the encrustation over
that which would leak raw
if allowed to flow openly.
The compassionate body
actively healing self.
In experiment,
I take off the fresh skin
and let the wound weep.

Mysore Sunset

A chameleon blush
across the sky adorns me
in warm fire.
Receiving the gift
I feel truly beautiful.
I embrace it, enfold
the colour
and dance unabashed
like an untouched child.
Catching the last
of the sun's sensual fingers
in my dupatta
I paint myself anew
in my lover's trailing embrace.

Liars

Asu Tears

Uske aako me hai pyar ka samundar	In my beloved's eyes there is a sea of love
Uske aako me hai pyar ka samundar	In my beloved's eyes there is a sea of love
Ab malum hua	Now I realize
Hum bilkul dubgai thay	We were both completely drowned
Mere dil me koi cheez nahi	In my heart there exists nothing
Mere dil me koi cheez nahi	In my heart there exists nothing
Sirf uski tasveer	Except the image of my beloved
Ab malum hua	Now I realize
Rat mai, maray aako mai	At night, in my eyes
Asu attay hai	Tears come
Ab malum hua	Now I realize
Meray aako kay asu	The tears in my eyes
Chatay hai	Desire to join
Uskay aako kay pyar ka samundar	The sea of love in my beloved's eyes
Ab malum hua	Now I realize
Hum bilkul dubgai thay	We were both completely drowned

Love Lies

Bleeding,
sundoor red
as the air ricochets
a thousand silent deaths,
the faint-hearted
walk away.

The Meeting Point

Skin dark, shadowed with memory, eyes vacant, lost, you slouched
towards the back of the terminal, your jaw lazy, chewing gum.

It took some seconds for me to recognise you.
You looked different from your picture.

In the flesh you were less vital, less thoughtful,
and walked slowly, as if you aged with every step.

You came over, embraced me briefly, I, who
was all dry mouthed and nervous smiles. In your arms

I sought your heartbeat, thinking it would match
my techno rhythm, but felt nothing but a regular

beat. I had changed on the plane; carefully picked
midnight blue silks, now creased,

shimmered violently against your subdued tones.
We journeyed through the airport's surreal steel

and chrome. Disorientated, I felt thirst and looked to you.
I had no currency and you no hard cash. You pushed

me towards a fast food outlet and instructed me to ask
in my 'nice British accent'. I did, and for the first time ever

my Black Britishness was rewarded. With a beaker full of water
that I was too nervous to drink, but thankfully occupied

my shaking hands, I walked beside you,
my dupatta trailing, dusting the floor.

You stopped near a native piece of art.
I touched its stone coolness with my fire skin, felt calm

in its presence. It was a deity, part man, part fish.
I embraced it. Hid my shyness behind a carved curve

and took a moment to give thanks, pray, for the blessing
of finally having you near and tried to push away doubt.

You had oozed passion via email and phone; now at the meeting point
where hypertext dissolved into flesh, you stood, silent. I felt your gaze.

It was as if I were being scrutinised by prospective
in-laws. But then, I suppose ours was an arranged liaison, of sorts.

The elavator was worst. Mirrors everywhere. Nowhere to hide.
I tried to become smaller and burned under your eyes.

En route to the car park we stopped at a small water garden
with its native totem. I found it beautiful. An auspicious welcome,

a recognition of the true belonging of the land. You scoffed
cynically. Said it was a touristic ploy to lull naive innocents

like me to think Canada to be truly a land of freedom
and democracy. In that moment you were illuminated.

We drove in silence and I considered
your distinct lack of enthusiasm, excitement or rush.

It was as if you had just picked up an object that you already knew
to be yours. The city lights before us, the rain falling, cleansing,

offering the city fresh and new; downtown deserted, you drove
into the heights of Stanley Park and switched off the lights.

I watched the moon on the Pacific as you watched me.
'Does the moon seduce the ocean or the ocean the moon?'

I asked, and when you replied 'The moon,
The moon seduces the ocean', I smiled

because in that moment, the girlchild in me felt you
were real, that you were true, though not warm

but cool. I glowed with the pleasure that you understood
the moon as I did, and I felt better about your steady heartbeat.

Three Photographs of You

One eye bigger than the other,
creases like rays of sun beam
from the corners of your eyes,
a dimple on the temple,
where cold metal had fired into your skin.

A generous nose held by half
moons of cheeks, thin slices
of ripe mango lips. Your chin cupping
a wave of soft silverblack hair
that laps against your face.

One coy ear, another that flaps
and waves for attention. A sparse
head of hair shorn short, whispers
of eyebrows, fleeced shoulders
and neck haloed in a zipped polo.

Your cancerstick is out of shot
but the fumes, visible, rise
like intoxicating incense
and fill the frame.
This is a rare image of you
in the moment, peaceful.

Proof in black and white,
evidence of the gaze
we exchanged, my eyes
through a lens on you, your eyes
captured, taut, still, outside
the house off Commercial Drive

where we first made love
in the yard where we ate
French cheese, Turkish bread,
red grapes, smoked BC's finest
and drank Indian tea.

2

Blurred,
but clearly defined, an ear
visible, almost as if you
are actually listening.
Your obstinate nature
held in Moghul profile,
your eyes masked,
hiding the battle within.

Looming over me, the sky's
ambivalent around you, your eyes
hidden behind dark glasses,
the collar of your fleece frames
you in a Count Dracula cape,
your T-shirted torso red
underneath. Your face
heavy with beard, shadowed
in agitation. Your lips open,
releasing an invisible volcanic flow.

Later that day, you shaved for me
by the ocean as I stretched
out on the fallen redwood tree.
When you came to me
you were unrecognizable,
your face unmasked.
I blinked in the bright white light
and for a moment as you bent
down to kiss me, I saw
my father.

Salt Spring to Vancouver, BC

Dreaming of baths we hitched
from the wilderness, blessed
in the back of open trucks
feeling the rush of life.
Three straight lifts then
bang, back into
the heart of
the city.

Locked out, we set up camp
in the yard, focus
of an emergency
neighbourhood watch
meeting – Agenda Item One:
the two Indians camped
out on the lawn.
                        Braving stares
we spent lazy hours
stinking like skunks, eating in
cheap cafes with spacious wash
rooms. Waiting for keys, we danced,
sang Louis and Ella
duets in the moonlight.

Close Encounters I

Dressed in black by you,
holding flowers of my choice –
white star lilies –
I cross the threshold
into your parents' sparse
2 up 2 down town house,
where the pale Aga Khan
smiles his benevolence
from every room.
Your parents do not smile

but make tea. We sit stiff necked
and take sips, as if we were English.
Offering biscuits, your mother
cross examines me. 'How much
do you earn?' I am amused. You burn
me with your eyes and answer
for me. Your father cuts to the chase
'What can you teach our grandchildren?
You are not Ismaili!'
I look towards the Aga Khan and answer:

'To be compassionate, fearless, loving, respectful,
courageous and to find humour in the ridiculous.'

Close Encounters II

The next day I found the lilies
stuffed into a suffocating vase
their abundant scent anointing
the room. Your mother heated
yesterday's dhal as I watched
you move Gulliver-like around
your parent's home. 30+ years
of marriage, double income,
an only child and what did they
have to show? A tiny, spartan
house, twin single beds, and whispers
of dollars stashed in a secret
bank account, awaiting 'a rainy day'.
And a son, who brings home an 'infidel',
and talks of freedom, love and choice.

Close Encounters III

Inside your parents' home,
a place where the sun
could not reach nor warm,
it was arid, barren, worn.
Here 20 years had passed
with the blinds drawn.
No music ever played,
as your mother suffered
from constant headaches.
Shoes hugged the front door
while our slippered feet moved surreptitiously.

In this house joy was held
tight in a fist, nothing fed or nurtured
but plastic plants grew miraculously.
Dust seeped through cellophane covers,
and the cooker continued to collect grime
despite its careful, foil skin.

But the surprise for me
was your parents' room
where Vegas was
recreated, kitsch and opulent.
Here, in whispers you told
me how 'they' slept side by side,
all these years, and how
your father complained,
that he'd never seen 'any action'.

Your mother, instead, preferred to do
her accounts in between the sheets,
taking careful notes
of all deficits, keeping check
in the room where risks were
never taken and money, like intimacy,
could be ill afforded.

Your father's gambling
days were long
gone. These days
he took to hedging his bets,
reading Western philosophy
as well as The Quran.
Your mother, forever vigilant,
maintained caution,
and ran a household where
the glasses were forever
half empty and reckless
hearts were disciplined
with short, sour measures
of maternal love.

Close Encounters IV

Your room,
a shrine to past lives;
the dead woman's
clothes hang in your wardrobe,
her books erect on your shelves
the knick-knacks bought
in Jaipur, carefully arranged
recently dusted. Dry
-mouthed, but curious,
I looked for photographs,
voice silent,
too scared to ask.

Charity

In the picture,
you are no more
than seven, captive
in your mother's
arms, held, to look
like an embrace;
your hair slicked back,
your tall, skinny boy's frame
suited in the shame
of a Salvation Army
shop-bought suit;
your mouth open,
fighting
for air.

The Jamat Khanna
(Burnaby, Vancouver, BC)

Stone silent, marble cold
your Jamat Khanna
quietly tasteful. Peaceful,
was not how I felt when
I tried to open its doors,
a house of God
with exclusive restrictions
on entry. I hold
the wrong name,
the wrong creed,
the wrong history
to be deemed worthy
to worship with you,
meditate and share,
the benevolence
of your God.

The Gudwara
(Burnaby, Vancouver, BC)

Within half an hour we reach
the Gudwara. Five blocks
away from your Jamat Khanna.
A house of God

where no-one is refused.
We sit humbled, equal
before God and meditate
as the woman Granthi reads

from the sacred Gurbani.
Later, after sweet offerings,
we share a plate of roti, dhal
and kheer served by the hands

of a brother devotee. As we
leave, a prayer is ending
and the Granthi intones
in soft, sacred Punjabi,

'God is within, God is without.
All Gods are one, one are all Gods.
There is no place free
from God. Truth is eternal…'

Still Life

Yours was a hot wound
piercing flesh through flesh,
an apologetic entry and exit

diagonal from temple to jaw.
The tiny tornado of steel,
with my name incompletely

engraved on its body, shot
through you, into me. Left me
kneeling, bleeding, but not yet dead.

Light Relief

The women of your fantasy are as diverse as you are inconsistent.
There is the woman who dances like a courtesan
but whose modesty is as dark as a hijab.

There is the woman who can cook Thai, Italian and Indian,
with equal flavour, fragrance and competence.

There is the woman who speaks fluently in English, Punjabi,
French, Spanish, Urdu and Hindi.

There is the woman who, in private, converses eloquently
on all topics, but in public never poses a challenge.

There is the woman who dresses conservatively, but creatively –
and exclusively – in cotton and silk.

There is the woman whose well connected
father can take you places.

There is the woman who turns over and offers herself,
whose legs stretch with accommodating yogic competence.

There is the woman whose eyes do not demand that you seek hers
and whose voice does not ask that you call her name and no other, whilst
'in the act'.

There is the woman who never asks you to go down on her,
but who goes down on you without question.

There is the woman who slips effortlessly into the dead
woman's clothes that hang in your wardrobe.

There is the woman whose energy is dictated by yours; who will rest when you rest, run when you run, and play, whenever you are in the mood.

There is the woman who never questions your relationship with your parents and why, in your late 30s, you still live at home.

The women of your fantasy are as diverse as you are inconsistent, and you demand me to wear them, like the dead woman's clothes

in your wardrobe. But did I not mention: last season's look has never been my style, and crushing my esteem

so that it fits into your rhythmic, lubricated palm, never my desire, fantasy or fashion.

The Package

Arrived rudely. 8am,
Saturday morning,
the intercom screaming

for attention. A box
wrapped carefully
in brown paper;

an old bag, recycled.
The long white label placed
squarely in between red

borders with
perfect squared-
off corners.

Par Avion glued in blue,
a sign of the skies
that bore this offering

from you. A box,
small enough to fit
old letters, new shoes

that pinch or a dead bird
that you bury
in the garden and grieve

lightly for. A Small Packet
— *Petit Paquet* stamped
on a pale green customs

label, that you valued at $50.
A tick in the box marked
gift/*d'un cadeau*.

Lines agitating paper,
marks signposting a journey,
a paid passage for unfinished

business. The Canadian Post
Corporation did their duty
and delivered.

I knew it was from you.
Your name, a sly yawn,
trying to escape

the page. My name
legible, formal
abrupt.

I wonder: when
you wrote, was it automatic
or laboured? My name,

two syllables intoned
as I taught you over the phone.
A name that you whispered

the night you asked me not
to leave you, the night you kissed
me into the music of our names

entwined. I tore through
our names, destroying the immaculate
paper layers and labels,

anxious to get within,
but knowing that I would
find nothing other

than shoes, papers and other stray
lost things. You forever
pragmatic, tying up loose ends.

Small Things

Small things irritated you:
nail polish, dyed hair, synthetic
fabric, voices raised too high
in laughter and holding hands.
Spontaneous trips, that hadn't been
well planned. Things left to the last
minute. Details that had not been
paid attention to
in the heat of the moment. Unplanned sex,
the mess from a woman's body,
unruly body hair,
oral sex. Small things
perhaps, but hugely significant all the same.

Snowflake Flutterfly

I

You
are the blackgold of the sun
that filters through
and catches
the snowflakes
in my hair.

I
glitter into pieces
in your refracted light,
become a jaded rainbow
bleeding around the moon,
a pregnant whole,
belly taut,
silent expecting.

What waters flow
here? Ancient
underground rivers dry up
lose voice,
like the Effra
secreting through
South London.
I wander
aimless
my unknown self
screams itself hoarse
not in the smooth, death wonder
of the night
but in the sharp life of day.

You are chaos,
a havoc of soft water,
but you only trickle tantalizingly
across my drought ridden body,
marked by unforgiving
journeys charted
to territories unknown.
I drink, parched to the bone.

'My mistress's eyes are nothing like the sun.'
Seen. But,
you are the blackgold of the sun
and I am a child of the Mayans
and seek succour
under a helio intensity
that chars old skin
to reveal a whole
renewed.

II

My wings melt
(another one of my harebrained schemes)
call me Icarus if you must...
At least,
I caught your
your eye awhile.

III

'Flutterflies', your child word
for the brief, exotic beauties
with butter wings that melt
captive under a magnifying glass.
An offering,
to the sun that blisters you.

IV

A late bloomer,
only catching on when it's far too late,
I cocoon my ugly mid-teen crysalis
self, give way to a parturiency,
coax forth a painted self,
a stranger
that exhausts energy
with a magnetic passion.
I disappear
destined to be captured
someplace, somewhere
in a jar, pinned
wing by limb,
living, breathing evidence
of an exotic
fleeting passion.

Smoke Wings

In your dreams you had wings,
butterfly wings, wet whispers
emerging from a cocoon.

In your nightmares you fell,
wings aflame like the painting
you saw made in memory

of Hiroshima. In my life, you
blazed. The smoke of your wings
brought water to my eyes.

The Catch

Thief of my heart, you flew
from here to another isle, oceans apart.
Distant lands allure you
with scents of lily and vine fruit.

Yet, my love, the rich soil here is also giving,
fresh with food that grows plentiful,
which I will pick, clean and cook for you.
I will nurture your body, your soul.

Oh sweetest one, pray rest
your mind, be at ease, for I have left
the light on. The beacon shines hopefully
and you can see its flame bright

from whichever vessel you sail upon.
Come to me, moth-like,
and I will open my door. Notice
that I have laced the walls of this house

with fine silk threads that your fingers can touch
as you find your way to me blindfolded by the dark.
Inhale deeply, for I have doused our chamber
with sage to ward away the evil spirits

which chase your heart far from me.
On your downy pillow, I shower tiny droplets
of lavender to soothe you to sleep, and in the morning,
I will bathe you. Wash you down like a babe

with the ocean sponge you brought for me,
souvenir from the depths of your maiden dive.
I will rejuvenate the coral imprints ingrained in your skin
with cat licks, draw out the salt that has settled

too long in your wounds. I will cleanse you,
anoint you with sandalwood, press you
to my oiled body and we shall be together,
safe in the tidal wave of love.

As sunlight escapes
across the woods next even-time,
we'll lie replete in rest
after a sleepless night of lovemaking.

At this moment I'll pull you to me. You sigh
and stir in languid contentment and I shall
take my left hand and draw from under my pillow
my mother's blade, her sacred *kirpan*,

and I shall fillet you like the prized fish you are.
As your lungs struggle like beached gills,
I shall watch the dead panicked stare
of your roe eyes. Your oiled skin

will glisten into a rainbow
as your exalted throes begin to shore towards a dying tremor.
I will know that you can no longer use my heart
as idly as a seashell whose captured, ecstatic waves delight

you awhile, after which, discontent, you toss it back
into the sea from whence it came. As I deliver your body
back to the ocean for her to claim, I shall remind myself
that there are plenty more fish in the sea.

In Between Days

In between the days
I am waiting
for the rain to stop,
the fruit in my kitchen ripens,
then rots. While the clothes
in my wardrobe
wait for me to lose
weight, the novel
inside me waits, while I
try to unblock
my fear. My womb
waits to be filled.
My insomniac self waits
for sleep to come.
In between days
waiting,
buses arrive,
planes take off;
summer comes and fades.

Conjurers

The Weight

Ours was not an overwhelming passion, like the tidal waves
I was used to.

Ours was an awakening. A sunrise
and sunset.

A steady unfolding,
like a flower; a tulip,

which bows,
             humbled
                       by beauty,
                                 abundance.

Tidal Moods

There are clear, still moments
luminous as an African sky
at night or the sea
when she calms
when I wonder
what governs me,
whether this centrifugal pull
is from a source rooted in the moon,
stars or simply hormones;
whether the magnet
moon is in cahoots with my seratonin –
or perhaps my seratonin seduces
the moon with the promise
of eternal, ecstatic bliss.

Father Figure

Faded jeans with a shadow
on the back pocket,
remembrance
of where your wallet and glasses
have been. A smile which fits
into all corners of your face.

A sly touch
of my breast which leaves me confused
in my innocence, not knowing
how much I should know
the sensuality
of your wily fifty-seven year old frame.

When I look at your face,
a face that I could look at forever
I do not understand
whether it is the father
I never had
or the first love I lost that I see.

The Transformation

(Stockholm, 2001)

Spring, I am told, is scheduled
for May 18th. We all wait
for someone to pull
the magic switch
that will green this city.
Outside my room: lithe yogic trees;
next door, a thin young man
who wears black,
listens to dull song
and makes long phonecalls
puncuated with a loud Ja! Ja! Ja!

Last night, it happened.
Today the Sylla reach
outstretched, open, open!
Like a book that reads
Joy! Joy! Joy!
Swedes open up like coy fans,
shrug off winter and reveal
bare flesh to the sun
who rewards worship with art,
a grand collage
using a transparent sheet of gold
that covers all shades of pale.
We now glisten and shimmy
confident in our new attire

The Flow

Like rivers to an ocean
we have known each other.
Life times swell, break
and merge again;
with every heartbeat
we sail closer

It is not about love
lost or broken
or a hurt that remains,
but rather an opening,
a lifting, a drawing closer
with every breath

I have known you;
your hips fit into mine,
we walk in step.
Across a myriad
of crowded rooms
our eyes meet

I was once your daughter,
you were once my child
and I left you
like an ocean leaves a shore,
and you, like a river,
cannot refuse this eternal flow

Surya

Under chlorophyllic cathedrals
oozing soft green light
we marry with shadows,
surrender to fingertips
of sun and lover's kisses.
This day I give in
and take a new lover:
Surya. As I turn to embrace
him, I don't know where you begin
or he ends, nor which is my true
beloved's touch.
All I know is that I wish
to be on fire, in union
with flames, and to this
I surrender.

Pakeezah – Pure of Heart (Urdu)

Incomplete, damaged, I continued
until she came my way, all smiles,
happy that I might choose

to love her. Called herself Pakeezah,
and in a Gregory Isaac stylee,
became '*nightnurse*' to my wounds.

Hers was a lighter-fuel love to the bonfire
of my damp soul; it took her flesh to warm
through where my heart had chilled

and stilled. Frozen heart wounds, blood
arrested by Allah's hand, I surrender
to a design bigger than I. Who am I

to argue fate? There are those who offer
pain like a seat on a crowded bus,
and those who receive humbly, sit and suffer.

She took up residence in the seat beside me.
In her arms I renewed, became bolder,
at her breast I suckled. The wound hungered,

I sought transfer of flesh, a suture.
She seemed abundant enough, ideal
in her openness. I feasted. Lightly at night

I chewed on succulent heart meat, flesh
so tender, raw, unashamedly pure. I became.
When on occasion she touched her breast,

murmuring pain, I would lull her with sweet
everythings and hold her in rockabye arms,
distract her with promised futures that dazzled.

Calmed, she settled, hands behind her head,
her soul cage wide open. How could I resist?
It is not my fault that she fed me so unwittingly.

I have no blame.
Some are meant for sacrifice, to be scarred,
then devoured, dancing naked through flames.

Encouraged by my delight she offers even more
love. How easy she is to take! No challenge.
Easy game. Fully recovered. Bored. I look away.

Naatch

Dancing on broken glass like *Pakeezah*,
with blood trickling from my *mehndied* feet,
eyes watch me, *chakar* after *chakar*
spinning as if I alone hold
the axle of the world
in the balance of my heels.
As my toes touch shards of hope
I take the weight
and I weave it into the momentum
of my Sufi *khatak*, flamenco
naatch.

Jealousy

Silence
like the gaps   between
empty chairs now sits
in our mouths.

Audre Lorde said that eye-
to-eye, sister to sister,
woman to woman,
there is so much
anger left unspoken.
All I remember
is that as I grew,
you tried to make me
smaller.
When I flew,
you weighed me
down. And when I was weak,
you rubbed salt into my wounds.

I did not know how
to leave you then,
but I know the moment
I chose something for myself
You
left
me.

Release

If the truth be known,
I would not love you now.
I would not let my love
wrap itself around you,
I would not give you that.

You know what I want?
You know what I really want
to do to you?
Fuck you,
fuck you

so hard that you feel
me tunnel deep in you, inside
out, rub you,
until you run an ocean,
your want, a honey-

sweet nectar, I,
a caramelled diver
plunging your fragrant depths,
my tongue reaching for your pearl.
We synchronize, swim mermaid-like

until you pull your hips down on mine
align these thighs
and tug,
        and ride,
                and tease,

and I wait for you
to come
to say no more,
and then I can
release.

Sunkissed

Rare sunshine ripens me
sweet as Valencia oranges

Vibrant kisses hopscotch
across my skin

Under the warmth I take myself
to a place where sunlight is not so

fleeting

The 4:10 Bangalore to Mysore

The sweet *khushboo* memory
of marigolds, oranges and jasmine;
the lilting *awaz* of college girls
singing in the *bhir* of the 4:10 ladies' compartment
from Bangalore to Mysore; Muslim girls
conjuring up school intrigues;
laughter like gentle waves skimming
from seat to seat; black *burkas*
etching out slender charcoal frames,
which as heat and comfort seep
in are stripped off to reveal
a feast of wild, true colour underneath.

She lays her head happily tired upon glass blue wrists
that create a music each time the carriage halts.
Her fragranced hair sheens in the sunset
and the faded flowers in her hair attempt
a last valiant resurrection. As the burning
sun melts across her face,
she becomes fire.

I want to take you in my arms,
pluck the flowers gently from your hair
and smell your true scent,
lick the sweet musk sweat from between your breasts
and whisper answers to all the questions
your latent body yearns for.
Tell me, woman of fire, will you listen?

Coke Break

I drink **Coca-Cola**® only when I travel in hot countries. It aids
my contest with the sun; a fast sugar fix empowers when I deplete.
Coke, a colonizing taste that quenches all colours
of tongues. **Coca-Cola**® the brand with a flourish of calligraphy,
a decorative swirl that emblazoned across my childhood days.

I am hugging her curvaceous, sugar-black body to myself, bursting her
open, licking her rim, lips sucking a firm glass top, a perfect O;
running my hands up and down the glass, working her
into a froth. She gushes abundantly, my lips catch the flow…
Coke is it. Always **Coca-Cola**®

Thieves

An Elegy for Two Boys

In tribute to Ricky Reel, Stephen Lawrence and their families

I

Ruptured concrete suburban skin
leaks poison that is paved within.
Feet sweet against the sting,
you're cushioned sole up.
Your fingertips trace
the A-Z veins
and change the cartography
of the metropolis.
Have travel card will travel
zones 1-6 — the world
your oyster, but London
killed you.

II

It was like any other day.
Nothing unusual, just the same;
walking to the bus stop/walking into town...
after a while it's a blur
kingstonelthamkingstonelthamkingstoneltham
nothing unusual, just the same
nothing unusual, just the same
It was my mate who saw them
he said '*RUN!*'
I said '*No! We haven't done anything wrong.*'

Battery acid tongues siren
their unavoidable existence.
Internal morse heartbeat screams: *FLIGHT!*
Trained feet seize up in a fit of dignified pride.
Thoughts like, '*but they're as human as me*'
translate into reasoning syntax
that escapes like gas
into the dense onyx sky and zeros
into the void between their eyes.

A breath later
you are running like the hunted.
A breath later
you are kissing blood into water.
A breath later
you are kissing blood into concrete.

IV

When it comes it's not like the movies.
When it comes it's like a joke
because you can't believe that it's happening for real, you know?
And I didn't see my life flash in front of my eyes
I just heard my mother's voice
'*Ricky beta... tu kider gay-a? Mai karh tinu ureekdi hai...*'
I just heard my father's voice
'*Stephen, son... where you go? Me still waiting at the door for you to come home...*'

Waiting in Vain

(London, Summer '98)

We wait for justice
in a summer that never came,
watch pale bodies
coutured in designs of silence
preening in apathetic
sound-bite frames.
The wheels of legality croak and whine
as a belated enquiry into life
young
lost
resounds hollow with the brazen
'I don't remember…'
From self-styled Tarantinoesque,
monosyllabic M.I.B.,
the essence of new Brit cool,
suited and booted
with intent to kill;
living *Eastender*, *The Bill* lives,
confident that the scales of justice
cast enough shadow
under which their youth
-ful, white selves can hide.

Partition Sketches I
(zool)

A single line
idly placed on a napkin
fifty-six years ago

A seismic fault
that continues
to tremor

Partition Sketches II
(zool)

May, in a modest flat in Sollentuna,
a group of learned Indian and Pakistani
men meet and excavate the details.

Waverley, Gandhi, Jinnah, Nehru
and Mountbatten bounce off the walls
in their retelling of the past

that created the present.
Families and fortunes torn
apart in relation to the paper

boundaries that poisoned the land
with li(n)es.
Fifty-six years later and the letters

studied for in Indian and Pakistani
universities account for worthless paper
degrees, that turn exiled, educated men

into part of the Swedish worker masses
who now philosophize on the independence of India
as the May 1st evening draws to a close.

Skafferiet i Ekoparken
(Stockholm)

A little girl in pink
watches me, no more
than five years old.

She has already learned
not to smile back when I look
up from my book and smile.

She holds my gaze
steadily, and then walks away, cool,
uninterested. But looks back

with her eyes, I look down
and wonder, does she see me
as 'other'? Half an hour later

the light changes and beautiful
Swedish gay men gather in the sun.
Tales of the troubles of bringing bananas

through US immigration tickle my ears.
I smile and lean closer towards them,
my face lit up by the sun as one

man complains of Swedish Immigration,
where the more obviously looking Swedish
are waved through, but he is always stopped

and questioned. But he shouts at them,
'I am as Swedish as you!' His defiance
touches me and I try to imagine

shouting at the next UK immigration officer
who stops me when returning home.
'But it is safe to shout in Sweden; people listen,'

the man declares and I wonder if he heard
my thoughts. I want to join their conversation.
A flash of pink catches my eye.

The little girl is back, goggle-eyed.
I lean back and stretch, uncomfortable
under the glare

of the sun and try
to remember places
where I belong.

Kulturhuset, Sergals Torg

(Stockholm, Sweden)

I

We move carefully,
negotiating between the black
and the white, squaring
off the opposition,
lining up the captive men,
parading the deliberation
that can destroy an army,
bring a clergy to its knees,
and disappear a monarchy.

Today, I have a whole
empire in my hand;
my fingertips command
power. This is not
just a game, this is
my life that wiles
away the hours. This war
is art; this death, a displacement,
a sacrifice, that creates
the means to win.

II

There is democracy here:
young, middle aged, balding, longhaired,
clean faced, suited and shabby
gather together as men,
form silent, respectful circles
around the players,
like Gods, lost deep
in concentration, their purposeful
De Vinci fingers poised
over submissive pieces.

No refugee status;
all belong here,
nations united in play.
East Europeans battle
with the Middle East, India
with Pakistan, Turkey
and Sudan. All men
dream of checkmate. In quiet
conference, these men remind themselves
of other lives, transform
into Kings, Generals, Bishops and Politicians.
But I notice the pawns and wonder
where all the women and children gather
and what games they play?

The True Bear Tale

(Stockholm, 2001)

The Bear came
from the North
looking for a mate.
We were all sentimental
watching the TV
reading the paper,
willing it to settle,
find love.
For weeks it trekked;
we followed.
He travelled all the way down
South, almost crossed
the bridge.
And then, some trouble
with sheep; he had to be
shot. I cried. Dreamt
about him for weeks.

Welsh Postcard

In passing places
rain veils disappearing
seas in salty blurs.

Across the horizon, soft
focus humpback isles and tankers
heave with industrial poise.

Last Night a Poet Saved My Life

Gave me mouth-to-mouth
licked away the kiss of death
breathed into me a new voice
that whispered sweet nothings
until all bitterness evaporated away

Last night a poet saved my life
fed me a feast of sound, tantalizing lyrics,
draped me in song
lulled me into soporific dreams
that awakened me

Last night a poet saved my life
gave me the beat
that my faithless heart had skipped
stoked dying fires
quenched my endless thirst

Last night a poet saved my life
shouted secrets in riddles
illuminated beauty in darkness
wove infinite shadows
out of light

Last night a poet saved my life
Made love flirting with ears
Sound arousing my sense of taste
I mouth words
My fingertips caressing the page

Notes

From 'Folds of my Mother's Sari', pp.11-13

Ghur	raw, crystallized sugarcane
Dudh	milk
Bhang	cannabis plants

From 'Osmosis', pp.14-15

Paraat	large, round, wide, flat metal rimmed container.
Parathay	a folded chapati cooked in butter, can also contain fillings like methay or potatoes.
Dhai	yogurt
'Ki kar di hai?'	'What are you doing?'
Godi	lap
Methay	fenugreek
Shalwar	loose, roomy trousers worn as part of a Punjabi suit.

From 'Name Journeys', p.16

Rama and Sita: In the Hindu epic, *The Ramayan*, Rama was the eldest son of the King Dashrat. The king had three wives. One of the wives desired that her son be next in line for the throne. She arranges for Rama to be exiled. Rama takes his brother, and his beautiful wife Sita, into the jungle, where they live in the wilds for 14 years. During this time, Sita is kidnapped by Ravana, the Demon God, and held in his kingdom for many months. Rama eventually rescues Sita. On her return he accuses her of infidelity, stating that she could not have lived 'purely' with Ravana. Sita proves her innocence via trial by fire. Thus, in Indian society, Sita is held up as the archetypal 'perfect woman'.

aupadi: In the Hindu epic, *The Mahabharata*, Draupadi's gambling husband loses her in a bet to his cunning cousins.

His cousins then try to undress Draupadi in front of her husband and family. Draupadi prays to Lord Krishna to come to her aid. He responds by making her sari never ending, so that her body is never revealed and her modesty and honour is left intact.

From 'Refractions', pp.17-18

'Meray jhutay... Hindustani' etc. A well known classic Hindi film song, translating as: 'My shoes are Japanese, my trousers English, my red hat Russian, but still my heart is Indian...'

From 'Excuses for a Father', pp.19-21

Ravana   The demon god who kidnaps Sita in the Hindu epic *Ramayan*.

From 'Mysore Sunset', p.28

Dupatta   Long, wide scarf worn with Punjabi shalwar kameez.

From 'Love Lies', p.32

Sundoor   Vermillion sandalwood paste worn by married Hindu and Sikh women.

From 'The Jamat Khanna', p.46

Jamat Khanna The place of worship for Ismaili Muslims.

From 'Light Relief', p.51

Hijab   Headscarf worn by Muslim women to cover their head and face.

From 'The Catch', pp.58-59

Kirpan   A sacred dagger, carried by orthodox Sikhs.

From 'Surya', p.68

Surya   Hindu sun god

From 'Naatch', p.71

Naatch   Dance (Punjabi, Hindi, Urdu)

Pakeezah   Fictional female Hindi film character, now an icon. In the film of the same name Pakeezah dances on broken glass in order to prove her honour. Pakeezah literally translates as 'pure of heart'.

Mehndi   Henna designs worn in celebration at religious festivals and marriage ceremonies.

Chakar   A graceful khatak spin of 6/8 beats per second. Can also mean a long, weary journey or a rut.

Khatak   Classical north Indian dance form, from which the roots of Flamenco can be traced.

From 'The 4:10 Bangalore to Mysore', p.75

Khushboo   an intoxicating fragrance (Urdu/Hindi)

Awaz   noise/sound (Urdu/Hindi)

Bhir   busyness, crowdedness (Urdu/Hindi)

Burkas   modest, loose, Muslim dress which covers the entire body (Urdu)

From 'An Elegy for Two Boys', pp.79-80

Ricky, Beta...ureekdi hai...:   Ricky, son...Where have you gone? I am still waiting for you to come home... (Punjabi)

From 'Waiting in Vain', p.81

Eastenders, *The Bill*   Two British soaps set primarily in the working class areas of London.

M.I.B.   *Men in Black*, a popular Hollywood film which happened to debut in London during the summer of the Stephen Lawrence enquiry.

About the author

"My journey started in India, where I left for England in my early years, my tongue flowing with Punjabi and Hindi. Having washed up upon these shores my first generation self grew... immersed in a foreign tongue until memories of my umbilical tongue became diluted. Now I play with notions of home and projections of the self I am supposed to be, in a land where there are no true reflections of me... I play god...create...music where there is no voice."

Raman Mundair was born in Ludhiana, India, and grew up in Manchester and Leicestershire. She currently lives in Scotland, where she is Shetland Arts Trust Writer in Residence for the Shetland Islands. In September Raman will return to her post as Lecturer in South Asian Literature in English at Loughborough University.

A writer of poetry, prose, plays, and screen plays, Raman's work has been featured on BBC Radio 4's Women's Hour, Greater London Radio and the BBC World Service. Her poems have been published in *The Fire People* (Payback Press,1998), *Bittersweet* (Women's Press, 1998), and *The Redbeck Anthology of British South Asian Poetry* (Redbeck Press, 1999) and *The New Shetlander*. Her work has been used in teaching at The Open University, Florida International University, University of Aberystwyth, University of Portsmouth and Roehampton University.

She has been Writer in Residence in Stockholm, Sweden, Oxford, Maidenhead and Slough. She has represented The British Council as a writer, workshop facilitator, and performer in Namibia, Italy, and Sweden.

"She is constantly sensual...tempered by a delicate care for detail, a quality of consideration that engages in the philosophical in sometimes complex ways...

Her poems grow with her, spilling out on the streets, in her food, in her bed, and across the landscapes she inhabits... As she expands her own sense of the world, these poems, with their elastic mutability, have found a way to assume her shape and to beautifully capture the sensibilities of Raman Mundair. This is why I look forward to reading more of her work: I want to see where she will take her poems in the future."

Kwame Dawes

"Collective and individual pain is sung out in varying pitch and personae; joy is to be felt, poignantly,through expression. The high points of the book are most frequently female (poets including)... Raman Mundair."

Dazed and Confused, review of ***The Fire People***

"...Power dynamics and political events such as the Stephen Lawrence case, dramatized in an excellent poem by Mundair...some of the most exciting poetry being written in England today..."

Lauri Ramey, (Cardiff University) ***Conch Magazine***